Basketball

Marshall Cavendish
Benchmark
New York

This edition first published in 2010 in North America by Marshall Cavendish Benchmark

Marshall Cavendish Benchmark
99 White Plains Road
Tarrytown, NY 10591
www.marshallcavendish.us

Published in 2009 by Evans Publishing Ltd, 2A Portman Mansions, Chiltern St, London W1U 6NR

Editor: Nicola Edwards
Designer: D.R. Ink
All photographs by Wishlist except for page 6 Glenn James/NBAE via Getty Images;
page 8 Jesse D. Garrabrant/NBAE via Getty Images; page 10 Bryan Bedder/Getty Images; page 12 Jesse
D. Garrabrant/NBAE/Getty Images; page 13 Andrew D. Bernstein /NBAE via Getty Images; page 16
Timothy A. Clary/AFP/Getty Images; page 21 Bill Baptist/NBAE via Getty Images; page 23 Streeter
Lecka/Getty Images; page 23 Copyright 2008 NBAE (Photo by Garrett Ellwood/NBAE via Getty Images);
page 26 Copyright 1998 NBAE (Photo by Andrew D. Bernstein/NBAE via Getty Images; page 27
Copyright 2008 NBAE (Photo by Andrew D. Bernstein/NBAE via Getty Images

Library of Congress Cataloging-in-Publication Data

Gifford, Clive
 Basketball/by Clive Gifford.
   p. cm. — (Tell me about sports)
 Includes index.
 Summary: "An introduction to basketball, including techniques, rules, and the training regimen of
professional athletes in the sport"—Provided by publisher.
 ISBN 978-0-7614-4455-8
 1. Basketball—Juvenile literature. I. Title.
 GV885.1.G54 2010b
 796.323—dc22
                                        2008055992

Marshall Cavendish Editor: Megan Comerford

Printed in China.
135642

Contents

Basketball

▲

Top basketball players are spectacular athletes. They can leap high and react quickly to perform amazing moves.

Basketball is a high-scoring, action-packed team sport. Players pass, catch, and **dribble** a basketball (by bouncing it as they run) around a court. Each team scores points by shooting the ball through a basket that stands 10 feet (3.05 meters) above the ground.

A basketball team has as many as twelve players, but only five are allowed on the court at one time. A team's coach can switch players on and off the court throughout the game.

Different basketball competitions have different rules, but most games for adults are 40 or 48 minutes long and are divided into two halves or four quarters. This may not sound long, but play moves very quickly and most players are exhausted when the final buzzer ends the game.

Basketball is exciting to watch. The action is fast and intense. Millions of people watch North America's NBA (National Basketball Association) league and the Olympic games.

Basketball is also fun to play. Many of the top players are very tall, standing over 6½ feet (2 m). But you don't have to be a giant to play and enjoy the sport. Young players starting out can play a version of the game called mini basketball.

▲ Coaches often send in substitutes so one player doesn't get too tired. Don't be upset if your coach calls you off the court. There's a good chance you'll go back in later.

▼ The team in the white shirts is playing offense. One player bounces and controls the ball while his teammates move around so he can pass to them.

Scoring a Basket

▲ LeBron James is about to score a basket for the U.S. team at the 2008 Olympics. The ball must travel down through the hoop for a basket to count. The board behind the hoop and the net is called the backboard.

Nothing beats the feeling you get when your shot sails through the hoop to score a basket. Every player on a team needs to be able to shoot well. This means that shooting will be a large part of your basketball training.

Players learn to score with different shots. In the set shot, players stand still with their hands behind and slightly underneath the ball. They stretch their arms up and release the ball with a flick of their wrist. Other shots, including **layups**, are made on the move.

A successful shot can be worth one, two, or three points. To score a **three pointer**, you have to take your shot from behind a line on the court called the three-point line.

A shot from in front of the three-point line is worth two points during regular play. A **free throw** is worth one point. One or more free throws are awarded when the other team has broken the rules.

▶

A jump shot is a common shot in basketball. You jump straight up and release the ball at the top of the jump.

▼

You are 15 feet (4.6 m) away from the basket when you take a free throw. Other players from both teams stand around the edge of the key, which is marked out by lines.

Scoring Superstars

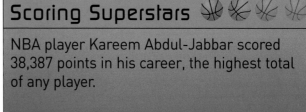

NBA player Kareem Abdul-Jabbar scored 38,387 points in his career, the highest total of any player.

In 1962, Wilt Chamberlain scored an incredible 100 points in a single NBA game!

The Court and Gear

Basketball can be played on an inside court in a gym or on an outside court in a park or school playground. The lines around the edge of the court are out of play.

A full-size court is divided by a halfway line. The half with the basket where your team scores points is called your front court. The other half is called your back court. The game starts at the halfway line with a **tip-off**. The referee throws the ball in the air and one player from each team jumps for it. This is called a **jump ball**.

If your team gets the ball in your back court, you have 8 or 10 seconds (depending on which rules you are using) to cross the halfway line. If you don't manage this,

▼ A basketball court is 94 feet (28.7 m) long in the NBA and 91 feet 10 inches (28 m) long in many other competitions. The shaded area is called the key.

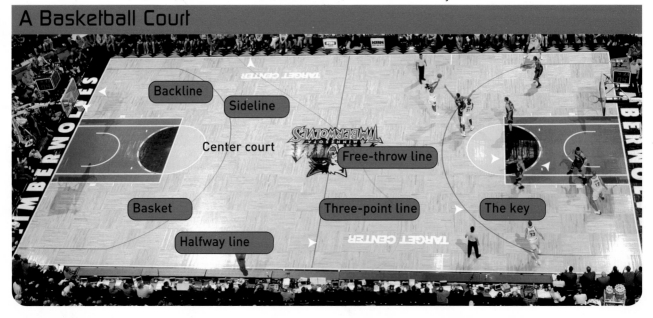

A Basketball Court

Backline

Sideline

Center court

Free-throw line

Basket

Three-point line

The key

Halfway line

the ball is passed to the other team. Once you move over the halfway line with the ball, you cannot return to the back court.

The basket, made up of a hoop and net, overhangs the court. On the floor below it is a rectangular area called the key. Players on offense aren't allowed to stand in this area for more than 3 seconds at a time.

You don't need lots of equipment to play basketball—just shorts, a T-shirt, and well-fitting sneakers. And, of course, a ball.

What a Basket!

The first baskets were real baskets used for carrying peaches. They were nailed to the wall by the sport's inventor, James Naismith, an American physical education teacher, in 1891.

In 1979, Darryl Dawkins slammed the ball so hard through the basket that the glass backboard shattered! He did this twice in three weeks, earning him the nickname "the Master Blaster."

▼
A basketball game starts with one player from each side competing at a jump ball. The ball is thrown into the air by the referee and both players try to tap it to one of their teammates.

▼
When the ball leaves the court and the other team touched it last, your team gets the ball. You put it back into play by throwing it in from the sideline.

Star Players

The world's top players are professional, which means they are paid to play basketball. In the United States, professional players are celebrities, just like film and music stars. Behind the glitz and the glamour, though, there is plenty of hard work.

▼ Los Angeles Lakers players Kobe Bryant (number 24) and Vladimir Radmanovic (number 10) compete with the Boston Celtics' Paul Pierce in the 2008 NBA Finals. The Celtics won the finals by four games to two.

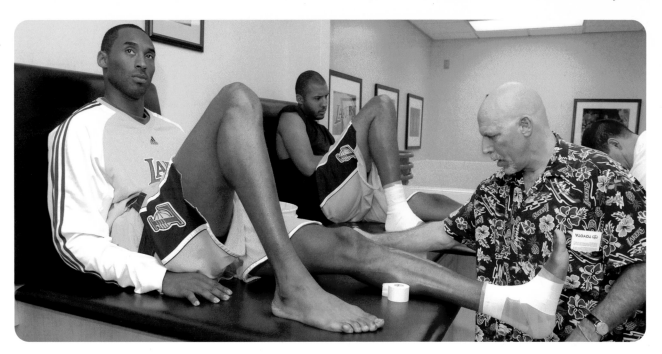

▲ Injuries can be damaging to a star player's career. NBA superstar Kobe Bryant sits on the treatment table as his team's trainer checks his leg. His ankle is taped to give it extra support.

NBA stars train hard and need to be incredibly fit. This is because they have a long and punishing season. The regular season begins at the end of October and lasts until April. In those six months teams play 82 games each.

The best sixteen teams then enter the playoffs from April to June. To reach the seven-game final for the NBA Championship, a team may have played as many as 103 games.

Trades and Pay

Players are sometimes traded, meaning they move to different teams. In 2007, Kevin Garnett was traded from the Minnesota Timberwolves to the Boston Celtics for seven other players, the biggest-ever NBA trade for a single player.

Kobe Bryant is believed to have earned $33 million in a single year, making him one of the world's top ten highest-earning sportspeople.

Along with games, training sessions, and drills, top players are expected to meet with fans and help promote their sport all over the world.

Passing

The best way to move the ball around the court is to pass it. You can pass the ball faster than you can dribble with it. Aim your passes carefully so that they are easy for your teammate to catch. The player catching the ball is called the receiver.

The simplest pass is the chest pass. You need to position your hands around the back and sides of the ball. Then you push the ball away from your chest. You flick your wrists as you release the ball to give it more speed.

▼ To make a chest pass, bend your elbows and then straighten your arms to send the ball flying away.

▼ To make an overhead pass, raise your arms above your head. Throw the ball forward with a flick of your wrists.

▼ The flip pass is a short pass that you make with one hand.

The **bounce pass** is useful when there is an opponent between you and your receiver. You bounce the ball past the opponent so that it springs up and into your receiver's hands. You can make a bounce pass with one hand or two hands on the ball.

Whichever pass you use, you need to be accurate. A weak pass may get caught by an opponent. If a pass is too strong, it might be hard for your teammate to catch. As soon as you have passed the ball, get moving! Your teammate may have to pass to you.

Try to catch the ball using both hands. Keep your eyes on the ball as it reaches you. As soon as the ball is in your hands, bring it into your chest. This protects the ball from other players.

▼ This player uses two hands to drive the ball forward and down for a bounce pass. Aim for the ball to bounce about two-thirds of the way to your receiver.

Individual Skills

▲ This player is in the triple-threat stance.

▲ Carlos Delfino of Argentina dribbles the ball and surges past Team USA's Jason Kidd at the 2008 Olympics.

With the ball in your hands, try to get into what is called the triple-threat stance. Hold the ball about chest high and stand with one foot ahead of the other and your knees slightly bent. Keep your head up to watch the court. From this position, you can do three things: shoot, pass to a teammate, or dribble the ball.

Dribbling takes a lot of practice to master. You use one hand to push the ball down to the floor each time it bounces up. Your hand must stay on the top half of the ball as you bounce it. Keep the bounce between waist and knee height if you can.

A **double dribble** is when you dribble the ball, catch it in your hands, and then start to dribble again. You don't want to do this, because the ball will be given to the other team. A player will restart the game with a throw from the sideline.

▲ This player dribbles the ball. He protects the ball by putting his body between it and his opponent.

▲ This player is pivoting. He steps around to the left to get away from a defender and to safely pass the ball to a teammate.

When you stop dribbling or when you catch the ball, you cannot run with it in your hands. This is called **traveling**. If you travel, the ref will give the ball to the other team. You can keep one foot still and twist or step around using your other foot. This is called pivoting and it allows you to turn to pass in any direction on the court. You can also use a fake to trick an opponent who is close to you. You can pretend to pass to one side, but pass to the other instead, or you can pretend to pass low and then shoot or start dribbling.

Playing Offense

Playing **offense**, or attacking, takes individual skills and great teamwork. Your team has to work together to get past the other team's **defense** and put yourselves in good positions to take a shot. If you have the ball, you have to stay alert and know where your teammates are.

When you don't have the ball, try to get into a position where your teammates can pass to you. This often means getting away from a defender who is nearby.

▼ The player in the blue jersey pretends to move one way before sprinting the other. He can then receive a quick pass from his teammate.

Basketball players make cuts, which are short, sharp sprints. Sometimes they drop one shoulder and lean one way but sprint in another direction to try to fool an opponent. Whenever you get free, look up at your teammate with the ball and be ready to catch a pass.

When a team is on offense, players try to get the ball in close to the basket for the best chance of scoring. The layup is another way of getting really close to the basket for a shot. This is when a player with the ball dribbles and drives toward the basket. Then the player jumps and takes a shot from close range.

Assists

Offensive passes that lead to a teammate scoring are called **assists**. John Stockton made a record 15,806 assists in his NBA career.

Magic Johnson made 10,141 assists in his NBA career. That's more than 11 assists per game!

In 1990 Scott Skiles made the most assists ever in a single game. He made 30 for his team, the Orlando Magic.

▼ To make a layup, you dribble the ball and step in close to the basket. As you leap up, you flick or push the ball up. You can shoot either straight toward the basket or bounce the ball off the backboard.

Playing Defense

Defending is all about stopping the other team from scoring and getting the ball back in your team's hands as soon as possible. It takes good individual skills as well as close teamwork.

There are different ways to play defense. When starting out, you are likely to guard an opposing player who doesn't have the ball. You follow his or her movements so that it is hard for your opponent to receive a pass.

If you are guarding the player with the ball, you need to get close to him or her. Bend your knees, face your

▼ Stay alert for a weak pass from the other team. You may be able to get the ball yourself. This is called an interception.

▼ Make yourself as big as possible when guarding the player with the ball. Your hands can be out to side if you think they will pass to the side. Be ready for a sudden change of movement or a shot or dribble.

▼ The defender (in white) sprints hard to keep up with her opponent. You need a lot of energy to run while playing defense. It is a very important part of the sport.

opponent, and stay on your toes, ready to move in any direction.

When the ball hits the hoop or the backboard it can bounce off at all sorts of angles. The skill of getting the ball in your hands at this time is called **rebounding**. You have to watch the ball and time your jump to get the ball before other players.

Rebounding is important in basketball. For the defending players, a successful rebound means they have the ball and can start an attack. For players on offense, winning a rebound means they get another chance to shoot.

▼ Yao Ming (*left*) and Aaron Brooks of the Houston Rockets both leap up for a rebound. To rebound successfully, you need to face the basket and time your jump well.

Team Plays

Players on a team work together on offensive and defensive moves. A team practices these moves in training so that they are smooth and successful in the game.

Teams work on ways of turning defense into attack. Your team may try a fast break. This is when one player dribbles and sprints up the court. Dribblers need support from teammates so they can pass the ball on the run.

Halfway line

▲ This complicated-looking move is actually quite simple. Called the full-court press, the team in blue closes in on the team in white to try to stop the players passing or moving the ball out of their back court. If the team with the ball stays in its back court for more than 10 seconds, then the ball will be given to the other team.

▲ Jason Kidd of the United States tries to defend against Spain's Pau Gasol during the gold-medal game in the 2008 Olympics. The United States won the game 118–107.

▲ Australia's Tully Bevilaqua calls directions to her teammates. Communicating with your team is important in a game.

Another simple team offensive move is the one-two pass. You pass the ball, then sprint hard past an opponent. Your team-mate passes the ball back to you when you are on the other side of your opponent.

At other times, you may work as a team to make space for the player with the ball. One or two teammates may move in one direction. These players draw defenders toward them and away from the player with the ball.

Basketball Rules . . . OK

Every sport has rules and basketball is no exception. Basketball's rules are enforced by a game's referees. They decide on everything, from which team put the ball out of play to whether a player has made a foul.

Before a game, referees check that players aren't wearing anything they shouldn't, such as jewelry. A referee starts and stops a game. A game is stopped every time the ball goes out of play or if a foul or a **violation** occurs.

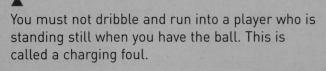

You must not dribble and run into a player who is standing still when you have the ball. This is called a charging foul.

You are not allowed to push or pull the shirt of an opponent. This is a foul.

▲
The player in blue slaps the hand of her opponent who is holding the ball. This is a foul.

Double dribbles and traveling are examples of violations. A violation is also called when the ball touches your feet or your team doesn't shoot the ball within 30 seconds (24 seconds in the NBA).

Basketball is a noncontact sport, so pushing, shoving, or tripping a player are all fouls. So is using bad language to other players or officials. When a foul is signaled, the player who has made the foul raises his or her arm. Referees usually give the other team free throws.

A player who makes five fouls (six in the NBA) is ejected. This means they are out of the game, although their team can use a substitute and continue with five players.

The World of Basketbal

Basketball is played all around the world at many different levels. Most of the world's basketball is run by the International Basketball Federation (FIBA). This includes basketball at the Olympics and the World Championships. Both competitions take place every

▼ Michael Jordan, one of basketball's biggest stars, soars through the air toward the basket. Jordan scored an incredible 32,292 points in his NBA career.

four years and have contests for men's and women's teams.

Professional basketball is played in approximately 30 countries. The most famous league is the NBA. It began in the 1940s and now has 30 teams in Canada and the United States.

The NBA is home to many of the world's greatest players. In the past, legends like Michael Jordan and Magic Johnson played in the NBA. Today's stars include LeBron James, Dwyane Wade, Kobe Bryant, and Allen Iverson.

While most of the players in the NBA are from North America, more and more come from around the world, such as China's Yao Ming, Manu Ginobili from Argentina, Spain's Pau Gasol, and Dirk Nowitzki from Germany.

The WNBA professional league for women began in 1997 and features 14 teams, all based in the United States.

Big Competitions

Only three of the NBA's 30 teams don't have names ending in the letter *S*: the Utah Jazz, the Miami Heat, and the Orlando Magic.

The first Olympic basketball final was one of the lowest scoring games ever. The outdoor court was muddy, it was raining, and the final score was just 19–8. It was the United States' first of men's basketball gold medals in sixteen Olympics.

▼ Lisa Leslie is one of the WNBA's most famous players. She was the first professional female to score a slam dunk. Slam dunks are spectacular shots made by players who leap above the basket and stuff the ball through the hoop.

Where Next?

These websites and books will help you to find out more about basketball.

Websites

http://www.ncaa.org/bbp/basketball_marketing/kids_club/
The kids' section of the National Collegiate Athletic Association basketball website. It contains video clips of basic skills, coaching tips, and fun basketball games to play.

http://www.hoophall.com/
This website tells you all about the players, coaches, referees, and supporters who have been inducted into the Naismith Basketball Hall of Fame.

http://www.harlemglobetrotters.com
The website of the Harlem Globetrotters. Watch videos of their tricks and learn all about the most famous show team in basketball history.

http://www.sikids.com/
Keep up to date with all the teams and scores from the NBA and NCAA at *Sports Illustrated*'s fun website especially for children.

http://www.fiba.com
This is the official website of the International Basketball Federation.

http://www.wnba.com/
The official website of the Women's National Basketball Association. The website contains lots of facts, profiles of the best players, and videos of the action.

Books

Dunning, Mark. *Basketball. Learn How to Put Speed in Your Step, Do the Drills, and Master All the Moves*. New York: Sterling, 2003.

Thomas, Keltie. *How Basketball Works*. Ontario, Canada: Maple Tree Press, 2005.

Basketball Words

assist A pass that leads directly to a teammate scoring a basket.

bounce pass A pass in which the basketball bounces about two-thirds of the way from the passer to the receiver.

defense Playing to prevent the other team from scoring.

double dribble A move in which a player dribbles the ball, catches it, and then starts to dribble again. A double dribble is a violation.

dribble Bouncing the basketball continuously.

free throw A shot from the free-throw line awarded by the referee for a foul by the other team.

jump ball A way of starting or restarting the game. A referee throws the ball into the air and one player from each side jumps for it.

layup A shot made from close to the basket.

offense Playing to score points.

rebounding Winning the ball after a failed attempt at a shot.

three pointer A shot that is worth three points because the shot is taken from beyond the three-point line.

tip-off The start of the game with a jump ball.

traveling When you take too many steps without dribbling after catching the ball. Traveling is a violation.

violation When one of the rules of basketball is broken. A violation is not as serious as a foul.

Index